HowExpert Presents

How To Start a Hot Dog Cart Business

Your Step By Step Guide To Starting a Hot Dog Cart Business

HowExpert

For more tips related to this topic, visit HowExpert.com/hotdogbusiness.

Recommended Resources

- <u>HowExpert.com</u> – Quick 'How To' Guides on All Topics from A to Z by Everyday Experts.
- <u>HowExpert.com/free</u> – Free HowExpert Email Newsletter.
- <u>HowExpert.com/books</u> – HowExpert Books
- <u>HowExpert.com/courses</u> – HowExpert Courses
- <u>HowExpert.com/clothing</u> – HowExpert Clothing
- <u>HowExpert.com/membership</u> – HowExpert Membership Site
- <u>HowExpert.com/affiliates</u> – HowExpert Affiliate Program
- <u>HowExpert.com/writers</u> – Write About Your #1 Passion/Knowledge/Expertise & Become a HowExpert Author.
- <u>HowExpert.com/resources</u> – Additional HowExpert Recommended Resources
- <u>YouTube.com/HowExpert</u> – Subscribe to HowExpert YouTube.
- <u>Instagram.com/HowExpert</u> – Follow HowExpert on Instagram.
- <u>Facebook.com/HowExpert</u> – Follow HowExpert on Facebook.

Publisher's Foreword

Dear HowExpert reader,

HowExpert publishes quick 'how to' guides on all topics from A to Z by everyday experts.

At HowExpert, our mission is to discover, empower, and maximize talents of everyday people to ultimately make a positive impact in the world for all topics from A to Z...one everyday expert at a time!

All of our HowExpert guides are written by everyday people just like you and me who have a passion, knowledge, and expertise for a specific topic.

We take great pride in selecting everyday experts who have a passion, great writing skills, and knowledge about a topic that they love to be able to teach you about the topic you are also passionate about and eager to learn about.

We hope you get a lot of value from our HowExpert guides and it can make a positive impact in your life in some kind of way. All of our readers including you altogether help us continue living our mission of making a positive impact in the world for all spheres of influences from A to Z.

If you enjoyed one of our HowExpert guides, then please take a moment to send us your feedback from wherever you got this book.

Thank you and we wish you all the best in all aspects of life.

Sincerely,

BJ Min
Founder & Publisher of HowExpert
HowExpert.com

PS...If you are also interested in becoming a HowExpert author, then please visit our website at HowExpert.com/writers. Thank you & again, all the best!

Table of Contents

Step 1: What You Need to Know to Get Started

If you've been thinking about starting your own hot dog business you already have an idea of the benefits. Being your own boss, making your own schedule, having flexibility, and most importantly having a recession-proof business are all reasons to consider a hot dog stand as a career.

Following are the other things you'll need to know about the business to get started:

- Potential earnings can be great because the profit margins on the items sold at a hot dog stand are HUGE. More than $70,000 a year is not atypical for a well-run cart in a good location.

- The initial capital required is not much. You can invest a few thousand dollars and have a profitable business in a month or two. It will cost about $500 to build a hot dog cart, or you can finance a new one with about a thousand dollars down payment, or buy a used cart for about three thousand dollars.

- You should also figure in up to a thousand

dollars for permits and licenses.

- We'll discuss the cost of inventory in another step because it varies depending on what you decide to serve.

- An alternate option is to buy an existing hot dog business. These average around $30,000 per cart but can go much higher in busy urban areas. Keep in mind that if you build your own successful business you can expect to realize similar profits.

- There are four critical items to a hot dog stand's success. The first is following proper food safety procedures. The second is having a good location. The third is serving tasty food, and the fourth is providing efficient service. We'll give you tips on how to accomplish all of these items in later steps.

With all of this in mind, it's time to move on to Step Two, the commissary.

Step 2: The Commissary

The commissary, while it's the step that is probably most unfamiliar to people who have never had a hot dog cart before, is the most critical step and must be done before you buy a hot dog cart.

In short, it's illegal to prepare food that's intended for resale in your home in most places. The reason for this is that other activities which occur at home can contaminate the food. For example, you may have pets in your home that enter the kitchen while you're preparing food and this is considered unclean. A commercial kitchen is supposed to be dedicated entirely to food preparation and therefore is supposed to be more sanitary.

(Some local health codes will allow you to modify an area of your home, such as part of a basement or garage, to fit their requirements and then you can skip this step. However, in most places, the commissary is necessary.)

Commercial kitchens that are intended to be used by mobile food vendors are known as commissaries. You will use this place to store your food and clean your equipment each day. Your board of health can give you a list of approved commissaries in your municipality.

Commissaries cost money and the fees vary. If there are a lot of mobile food vendors in your city, you'll have more options and the fees will be lower.

Another option apart from renting from a commercial commissary is to find a business that has a commercial kitchen that you won't compete with that may agree to let you use their operations for a smaller fee.

Examples would be day care centers, caterers, nursing homes, private clubs, etc. If you get someone to agree to this you can usually go back to the health inspector and get the commissary requirement waived.

It's crucial to deal with this issue and find a working commissary option first because where your commissary is located may affect where you choose to locate your cart. Don't buy a cart until you have a commissary picked out and approved by the health department.

Step 3: How to Find a Hot Dog Cart

To start a hot dog business, the most important thing you'll need to do is get a cart.

You must follow the following points step by step in order to make sure you don't have hassles with the health department later on.

1. Pick what city you're going to have your cart in. You don't have to have an exact location yet but it's important to determine the municipality before you buy a cart.

2. Visit the local health inspector there. Explain that you want to set up a hot dog cart and get a copy of the local health codes and any other relevant regulations from them. These codes will spell out exactly how your cart needs to be equipped. If your cart does not meet the health code you may fail inspection and it will cost you time and money, so get it right from the start.

3. Once you know precisely what you need to have on the cart, you can pick one out. Your choice is between a stationary cart or one with wheels which can be towed. We recommend for your first cart you buy the latter so that it's easily

moved if your location doesn't work out or if you find multiple locations that work better seasonally.

4. Don't buy the cart yet! Take the plans back to the inspector to have them approved. If you're buying a new cart, the manufacturer will give you copies. If you're buying a used one, the owner should have a copy. If you're building your own, you'll use the blueprints you're working from.

5. To buy a used cart, the best place to start is with local classifieds because the carts for sale there will meet the local requirements. If you have a good idea of what you need, you can also try eBay or look for hot dog carts for sale online.

6. If the health inspector approves the plans for your cart, you can purchase or build it. (To get the parts you need to build a cart, visit your local hardware store or purchase a kit online.)

The variables of a cart are as follows: fixed or hitched, size, and heat source. We recommend a medium cart to start out, and as noted above, hitched (the mobile kind) is best for the beginner. As for heat source, you'll need at least one twenty-pound cylinder and one spare.

The next consideration with the cart is the heat source. A medium sized cart should have at least one twenty-pound gas cylinder and one spare. Get a hose with a quick connector so you don't need a wrench to change cylinders.

The board of health will also tell you what you need on the cart in terms of hand washing equipment. Typical are a clean water tank, a tank for waste water, and a working sink with faucet. You may also need sneeze guards as a hygiene requirement.

Your cart will need an umbrella, which you can buy from a cart manufacturer, get from the reseller if you're buying a used cart, or you can pick a hot dog brand to affiliate with and then get it for free from them because it advertises their product.

The last thing you need is either a display case or coolers to put buns, soda, etc. in. The display cases look better but they're more expensive and more of a hassle so you may want to start with coolers and see how things go.

Now that you have a cart and it's properly outfitted with the essentials, we'll deal with the next important step – the paperwork.

Step 4: How to Get All the Paperwork Done

First, you'll need to incorporate, and then you'll need to deal with some requirements that are unique to the mobile food industry.

To incorporate, first you'll have to decide what type of business structure to use. You can be a sole proprietorship, a partnership, a corporation or an LLC. Sole proprietorships and partnerships have limitations on how you can transfer the business, and they also allow creditors to go after your personal assets if you are sued, so we don't recommend these options.

To protect yourself from this problem, you need to incorporate as an LLC or corporation. Speak with a qualified attorney and accountant to determine which form is best for you, and to learn what regulations they each come with.

After selecting a business type, you need to select a name for your company and register it with the state. Visit your state's website to search to see if the name you've chosen is already in use, because if it is, you'll need to pick another one.

Once you've settled on a name, it's time to incorporate. You can either hire an attorney to do this, use an incorporation company or do it yourself. An attorney is the best choice if you have the budget, but if not, sites like www.incorporate.com,

www.companiesinc.com, and
www.incorporatefast.com can help you.

It's possible to do it entirely on your own through your state's website, but we recommend spending the extra $100 or so to at least use one of the incorporation companies, as it will save you time and energy that you can better expend on other areas of the business. There may also be local regulations for business filing (on the state, county and municipal levels) so check with the respective websites to find out if you're not using a lawyer.

The board of health should be able to tell you what requirements you need to fulfill specifically for a mobile food business, and you can also get this information from your state website. For readers from the state of California, keep in mind that your state has the most complex food safety laws on the books anywhere and this is an area you will have to research carefully.

Beyond licenses and registering a business, liability insurance is the biggest legality you have to deal with.

Now that we've discussed licenses and permits, there's one more financial area you need to delve into...insurance. This will include liability insurance, which is required for food service businesses virtually everywhere, and depending on your locality, you may need other forms of insurance as well.

Liability insurance covers you if someone gets hurt from patronizing your business. At a hot dog stand, this could happen from choking, getting food poisoning, or being injured by your equipment. The good news is that liability insurance for a business like a hot dog stand is pretty cheap. Five or six hundred dollars a year is common.

You can check with your regular insurance company first to see if they offer food service liability insurance but it's not very likely that they will. However, either they or the health department will be able to steer you towards an agency that will be able to provide this type of insurance.

Finally, keep in mind that there are other insurance requirements you may need to fulfill too, depending on your state and municipality. Fire insurance may be required, you may need worker's compensation if you hire an assistant, and you might even need vehicle insurance.

We've spent a lot of time on this step because it's important and there are a lot of requirements, but now it's time to move on to Step Five, location, which is more fun.

Step 5: How to Find the Best Location

Location is the single most important component in your hot dog business. No matter how good your food is if there isn't an audience for it, there's no point. This is why we recommend purchasing a mobile cart for your first cart, so you can relocate easily if it doesn't work out.

Keep in mind that you can put your cart on public property or private property. Public property would be land that's owned by the municipality, county or state in which you place your cart. For example, if you put it in a park or on the grounds of a school, or on a sidewalk in a city, that's public property.

Private property, on the other hand, is owned by a person or a corporation. It may not occur to you that you might want your cart on private property, but when you think about the possible locations, you'll see some private ones are excellent options. For example, a strip mall or stadium is an example of private property.

First, let's discuss public property. The benefits to this are that you don't have to pay extra to place your cart and the permits you applied for should let you put the cart anywhere within the jurisdiction of the municipality.

To find a good public location, drive around looking for places where there are a lot of people on foot with sufficient room to place a decent-sized cart and a clear view so that people can see your cart from the distance.

Some possible good public locations:

- On a sidewalk near other restaurants. Keep in mind that they may not like you being there and may try to hassle you, but if you've got all your permits and pass health inspection, they can't do anything about it.
- An office park. In the current economy with so many layoffs, the people who are left don't have time to take long lunch hours. Putting tasty food within walking distance of them is very appealing.
- A university or large high school. You'll have a built-in audience that's on the run and happy to have an alternative to cafeteria food.

Obviously, the better the location is the more chance there is that there will be competition. On a street corner in New York City, for example, you might see three hot dog stands in a row. While there might be enough hungry people there to support all of this business, it can be frustrating to find the perfect spot and have imitators show up, and it can also be frustrating to set up where there are already stands and have the owners hassle you.

For this reason, the main advantage to private locations is that you can sometimes work out an exclusive arrangement to be the only cart there. The downside to this is that private owners almost always ask you for rent.

Here are some ideas for minimizing the effect of rent on your business if you go for a private location:

- Ask for a trial period where you can operate rent free to show the owner that your cart will actually draw in business.

- Work out a month-to-month arrangement so that if the location doesn't work out you can move on.

- Work out a deal on a corporate campus where the owners will be happy to have you there because it keeps the workers on the grounds at lunch time.

When you have your cart set up and are actually trying out the location, the best way to tell if it works or not is your daily intake. Your first few months of the business, $200 a day or so is okay, but by the time you get into a groove, you should be making at least $500.

A few other locations you'll want to check out for your business:

- Private developments with association pools (you'll have to get permission from the homeowner association or landlord if it's a rental)
- Any public recreation area like a beach, park, campground, etc.
- Industrial parks
- Flea markets or amusement parks
- Train or bus stations

Finally, consider that you may want to relocate the cart for special events like fairs or craft shows. The profits at such events are huge—they can be as much as a few thousand a day, and you can charge more than you do at your ordinary location.

However, it's a high-pressure environment where you have to be speedy and may best be saved for when you know what you're doing.

Now that we've discussed regulations, the equipment and location, it's time to think about the heart of the business—the food.

Step 6: Basics of the Food

The basics of the food you'll be selling on your hot dog cart are hot dogs, chips, drinks and condiments. While you may see other items served at hot dog carts, like sausage and peppers, there are two very good reasons to stick to food that you don't have to cook. One is speed and the other is sanitary.

Hot dogs, chips and soda are a lot easier to serve faster than food that has to be cooked. The faster you serve, the more people you can serve during rush hour and the more money you can make, so anything that cuts down on the time it takes to prepare the food is critical.

As for sanitary concerns, all of these items come prepackaged. Soda, buns and chips are purchased in sealed containers, and hot dogs qualify as prepackaged according to the board of health because they are precooked.

You don't actually cook hot dogs at a hot dog stand, or at home for that matter, you just heat them up. Sticking to items like this makes it much less likely that your customers will ever get sick from your food, and it also makes it a lot easier to deal with the board of health, who consider them non-hazardous and therefore regulate them less.

The basics also require fewer modifications to your hot dog cart. If you are cooking meat, for example, you'll probably need a hot water sink, which costs more and is harder to service.

Similarly, you want to keep it simple when it comes to condiments. Ketchup, mustard, and relish are the basics, and we don't recommend you go beyond that when you're first starting out.

Ketchup is the condiment that's most likely to turn because its ingredients are attractive to mold in hot weather. Keeping your ketchup in a squeeze bottle and putting that on ice on hot days should solve that problem.

Other items like mustard, relish, tomatoes and peppers that have a high acid content are naturally resistant to spoiling, so you should be fine with these. Onions don't spoil easily in a way that makes people sick, but they can start to taste funny or look funny in hot weather, so if you're going to serve them, check on them frequently.

Sauerkraut, chili and cheese may be expected at the hot dog stand but they can go bad and are therefore possibly considered "hazardous" by your board of health. Check with them to see how serving these items will affect your hygiene requirements.

Regarding "cooking" the food, if you stick to the basic items then we're talking about steaming hot dog buns and heating the hot dogs. The latter can be done either through steaming or boiling. Steaming takes a few minutes more but it produces a more flavorful dog and looks better to the customer.

Boiling is necessary if you're somewhere where the turnover has to be fast. To boil the dogs, fill a water pan with hot water, heat it until it's boiling, let them boil for about 2 minutes and then turn off the gas. You can cook around 25 dogs at once using this method, but if you leave them in the water too long after the heat is turned off, it leaches the flavor out.

To steam your buns, put an insert on a steam pan, put the fire on low, and put the buns on top of the insert. (You can steam dogs this way as well.)

To purchase food and other inventory, start out by joining a warehouse club (BJ's, Costco or Sam's Club). They sell hot dogs, chips, soda, condiments, and miscellaneous items like straws and napkins in large quantities. This will also allow you to try out different brands of hot dog and see which taste the best. Eventually, when you settle on a favorite brand, you'll want to order the dogs from a distributor.

Some of the top hot dog brands:

- Ball Park Franks
- Bests Kosher
- Hebrew National
- Louie's All American Kosher Hot Dogs
- Nathan's
- Red Hot Chicago
- Sabrett's
- Shofar
- Sysco
- Vienna Dogs

We recommend purchasing all beef dogs because they taste better and are less prone to causing foodborne illness than hot dogs which include pork.

When you're first setting up, you won't want to purchase more than two days inventory at a time so you don't waste food and don't put too much money into it up front. About 250 hot dogs and buns, 150 individual bags of chips, and ten cases of soda should do it.

When it comes to buns, there are a few different types. A bun slit on top is called a new England style bun, while if it's slit front to back it's an ordinary hot dog bun. Hot dogs also come with flavors on them like poppy seed or sesame seed. Some of these are popular regionally, so if your competitors are also using poppy seed buns, you'll want to get them too. Otherwise, start with the plain bun.

Besides knowing what to buy, you'll need to know a bit about food safety. The regulations covering food safety will depend upon your local and state governments, so we're going to discuss general good practices here.

What causes food poisoning? Most of the time it's bacteria, which is almost always caused by contamination from storing food improperly or using poor hygiene. (When it's not, it's present in the food itself from the time it leaves the packaging facility. You can't do very much about that except to have liability insurance.)

To avoid food spoilage from bacteria, you need to store your food at 40 degrees Fahrenheit or lower. These means you'll need a freezer and that you must throw out leftovers at the end of the day (they've been sitting around in warm temperatures and are more likely to harbor bacteria).

Improper hygiene, which when it comes to a hot dog stand means not washing your hands or utensils properly, is a much more common cause of food-borne illness.

Wash your hands frequently with soap and warm running water to avoid problems. Washing should take at least 20 seconds and you need to scrub and then dry your hands completely with a paper towel. Any time you do anything that could possibly introduce bacteria, including going to the bathroom, coughing, sneezing, handling garbage, touching raw food, touching someone else's hands, eating, drinking, or smoking, you'll need to wash your hands.

In addition, washing all flat surfaces and all containers and utensils on your cart will prevent contamination. Use hot soapy water and sanitize by wiping down with bleach.

Now that you know what food to get, how to prepare it, where to purchase it, how much to purchase, and how to ensure that you follow good food safety procedures, in the next step we'll talk about additional things you need to purchase.

Step 7: What Else You'll Need

Besides the cart and food, there are a few other things you'll need to set up shop. The first is two coolers for drinks plus one cooler for frozen dogs. We recommend buying coolers with handles and wheels because when they're filled up with soda and ice, they're too heavy to carry comfortably.

Your cart will come with a set of steam pans but you should buy one or two spare sets. You'll also need large serving tongs for the hot dogs (get at least two), serving spoons for condiments if you're serving anything that can't work in a pump jar, and a cutting board and knife for tomatoes or onions if you serve them.

We recommend large pump dispensers for the ketchup and mustard. You'll also want a folding table for the condiments (this lets the customers self-serve to the side so that you don't have to hold up the line putting items on for them), and a thermometer to check the temperature of the hot dogs.

You'll need paper bags, straws, napkins, and wax paper or tin foil to serve the hot dogs with. You'll also need cleaning supplies, including paper towels, a two-gallon bleach bucket, and bleach. You'll fill the bucket with water and add a capful of bleach in order to sanitize the surfaces of the cart, which you'll do whenever things get slow).

You'll also need at least two 5-gallon tanks for water. One is for bringing clean cooking water with you in the morning and the other is for disposing of the used cooking water at the commissary after you clean up. These should be clearly marked in order to avoid getting them confused.

You can get all of these items at your local warehouse store or a restaurant supply store, so shop around to find the best prices. Now that you've purchased everything you need and you should have your permits in place, we're going to talk about setting prices and collecting sales tax in the next step.

Step 8: How to Set the Best Price

Sales tax rates vary depending on your state. Almost all states do charge sales tax for mobile food carts. At the time this book was written, the exceptions were Delaware, New Hampshire, Montana, Oregon and Alaska. Out of the other states, rates range from almost 3% to more than 7%. If you're using an accountant, get the correct tax rate from him or her or find out on your state website.

Your municipality or county may also require that you pay local sales tax. The county clerk or city clerk will be able to answer this question for you.

When it comes to collecting taxes, there are two methods. Keep in mind that you have to charge sales tax on every transaction. You can either build in the sales tax to the price.

For example, if you intend to charge $1.00 per bag of chips and your state requires 7% sales tax, you list the price as $1.07. If you do this, you'll want to isolate the sales tax as you're doing the transactions. (In other words, keep all the sales tax in a separate container from your other cash flow.) This is fine if someone hands you seven cents along with the dollar, but more often than not you have to make change and this will slow you down.

The other option is to round up your prices slightly. Using our example, you charge $1.10 for the bag of chips and deduct the sales tax at the end of the day.

We recommend this method for a few reasons. The first is that it does go faster, and the second is that if you have a fractional sales tax amount, for example, 2.9%, it's impossible to collect the exact sales tax on each transaction.

Whichever way you decide to collect the sales tax, open a bank account just for that and make a deposit in it at the end of every day or the beginning of the next day. At the end of the month, you'll submit the tax to your state. You can get the forms and deadline for this from your accountant or from your state Department of revenue.

When it comes to setting prices, besides figuring out how you will handle the sales tax, you also always need to keep in mind the most important factor in customer satisfaction, speed. For this reason, we recommend setting prices in increments with quarters. This means that most of the time you'll only have to keep quarters around to make change.

As to what price will give you a good profit margin, you can find the sweet spot by visiting your competitors and seeing what they are charging. This will give you a range within which you can figure out your costs and your profit margin.

Don't forget to figure in additional costs when calculating your profit margin. It's not only what you pay for the hot dog and soda, you also need to figure in rent, licenses, advertising, etc. Keep your pricing flexible in the beginning so you can figure things out.

You may start with one brand of hot dog and switch to another that's either more or less expensive, and your other expenses may change as circumstances change. (For example, if you're really busy you may need to hire an assistant eventually.) Set a price and see if it's working for you and readjust if necessary.

Keep in mind you don't want to be either much more expensive than your competitors or much cheaper. If you're too expensive people will balk, and if you're too cheap they'll think something is wrong with the quality.

Finally, when you start out, you'll need to know how much change to have. If you have a hundred dollar bills, around twenty five dollar bills and a few rolls of quarters, you should be set. Now that you have everything in place that you need, in the next step we'll talk about how to organize yourself for a full day of business.

Step 9: How to Organize Your Business Day

In this step we'll give you a full run through of a day in the life of a hot dog cart owner, from setting up to shutting down and beyond.

Setup

1. The night before, prepare your condiments. This means filling your pump jars and making sure you have enough of whatever other condiments you'll be serving.

2. Stock your cart and coolers with hot dogs, buns, soda, chips, napkins, and wrapping materials. This should also be done the night before so if you find you're short of anything you have time to restock.

3. In the morning, tow your cart to your site. Unhook it from your vehicle and stop the wheels to keep it from rolling.

4. Put water in your steam pans and start the gas fire.

5. Put out your coolers.

6. Set up the condiment table.

7. Put out a trash can that is lined with a garbage bag.
8. Check to see if the water is boiling. If so, start cooking the dogs. (A hot dog that's fully frozen takes around 6 minutes to cook.) Also, check frequently to make sure that the water levels are high enough in the pans.
9. When business is slow, wipe your surfaces down with your bleach solution and empty the trash bag.

Serving

1. Take the order and add up the prices.
2. Serve the dog. Do this by using a tong to put it in the hot dog bun and wrap it in a wax paper sheet or foil.
3. After handing the dog to them take their money, give them their change, and then either give them the chips and soda or let them take it themselves from the cooler. (The former will cut down on inventory loss but the latter will save time. If you're going this route and letting

people serve themselves figure in a little inventory loss when you're trying to determine your profit margin.)

Closing Up

1. When you're ready to shut down for the day, close your umbrella to let customers know you're done.
2. Turn off propane and let the water cool off.
3. Pour the dirty water into the waste water tank for disposal at the commissary.
4. Take inventory so you know if you have to replenish anything.
5. Put everything loose back in your vehicle and then hitch the cart up again.

Now that you know how to organize your business day, you've got the basics of a hot dog business down pat. The next steps will tell you how to deal with the health inspector, which you'll have to at some point, how to advertise and market your business, how to increase your profits, and how to expand when you're ready.

Step 10: How to Deal with the Health Inspector

The good news is that this step is very simple if you've done your homework and followed the previous steps to a T. You should have a good familiarity with the health code and your cart and your practices should comply with it.

The health inspector is not trying to cause problems for you, in spite of what some people think. They're only trying to make sure people are safe. Don't act defensive because you should have nothing to hide. There are many good reasons to follow the food safety regulations listed in these steps and outlined in the health code. You want your customers to enjoy a safe meal and to keep coming back.

What happens if something goes wrong? The penalty for failing a health inspection depends on the locality. In most cases you get some provisional period during which you are supposed to correct the problem, and then you get re-inspected. To get closed down for an initial health inspection there have to be major violations that are truly dangerous, such as if rodents are getting into the food storage.

If you have followed the first steps correctly, you should have no problem with your health inspection. Your commissary will already have been approved, and your cart will have the necessary equipment such as a hot water sink if you're preparing true cooked foods. If your health inspector is really strict and fails you because of a mistake in food storage or shows up just when you've run out of hand soap, these minor errors are easy to fix in time for the next health inspection.

Now that you know how to keep the health inspector happy, in the next section we'll talk about how to keep your customers happy.

Step 11: How to Keep Customers Happy

Besides having good food, there are three components to keeping your customers happy. These are keeping the line moving, good service, and friendliness. In the right location, any hot dog stand with good food will do fine, but to succeed and get repeat business you need to keep these three things in mind.

People buying their food from a hot dog stand are in a hurry. They'll wait a bit during the lunch rush hour but their patience is limited. Here are some easy ways to speed up your line:

- Let customers serve themselves when it comes to condiments. Put all liquid condiments in pump dispensers and put them on a table beside your cart. You can also do this with the chips and sodas but as noted above in the step about food, this can cause inventory loss.

- Do the same thing with plastic utensils and straws. Taking time fishing for straws while you could be handing out dogs or making change is a bad idea.

- If you get caught up in a big rush, you can skip the step of steaming the buns. Steamed buns taste better, though, so do this only if necessary.

- Have a printed menu or display board with prices. This will save time with customers asking questions and can help them give you the right change.

- If your budget allows, have a helper. If you have one person cooking and serving food and the other person handling money, things go much faster.

- Fill your water pans every ten minutes. If the water evaporates completely, you'll need to refill entirely and heat it up again, and that takes longer.

- Always check to make sure you have enough water and propane with you before you go out for the day. Running out can ruin your lunch hour.

Speed is the most important component of service, but it's not the only one. Remember to be courteous to your customers. Saying please and thank you is a must, and if there's a dispute over change or what was supposed to go on the hot dog, it's a lot faster and easier to give in to the customer and you'll save money by saving time in the long run.

Finally, go the extra mile and try to be friendly. (If

you don't like dealing with people the hot dog business is probably not the right business for you.) Try to remember your repeat customers, smile every now and then and make small talk, even if it's just about the weather. People like to deal with the familiar, and if you're friendly they'll keep coming back.

Now that you know what it takes to keep your customers happy, in the next step we'll talk about how to find customers in the first place—marketing and advertising.

Step 12: How to Build Your Hot Dog Business with Marketing and Advertising

While it's true that a hot dog cart attracts customers almost automatically, that doesn't mean that you shouldn't give some thought to marketing and advertising. Marketing can be as simple as giving your hot dog stand a memorable name and having a logo printed on the menus and napkins so people remember you.

If you're going to go to this trouble, make sure your message is consistent and fits your market. For example, if you're going to place your cart on the grounds of a university where the sports team is called the Gators, you might want to call yourself Gator Dogs and get a logo with an alligator on it. This helps people remember your business, especially if you're in an area with a lot of competition. If so, you need a "hook" to stay in their brains.

Once you have your marketing message in mind, you can advertise it with printed materials like business cards, menus, and coupon books. All of these should feature your company name, your logo, and a slogan, and you should carry them around with you everywhere you go so you can make people aware of your new business.

You can distribute these in your neighborhood, put them on cars in the local parking lots, or hand them out to receptionists in office buildings. Also, consider regular promotional events like half-off Thursdays or buy two dogs and get a free soda. When people come to expect these, they'll make it a habit to check out your cart.

You can also consider advertising in the phone book or setting up a website, but unless you're planning on running a hot dog empire right out of the gate these efforts are probably overly ambitious. The best way to get customers to come back is to treat them well.

You might even want to consider giving people free samples when you're first setting up so they can try the goods before they buy. This is one of clear advantages to a hot dog cart over other businesses— pleasing your customers is so simple that you really don't have to invest in complicated marketing or advertising initiatives to make money. In the next step we'll tell you a simple secret to adding to your profits.

Step 13: How to Make Additional Income

This step isn't unique to hot dog carts but it does work particularly well with them. It's a simple way to add profit to your business while raising the costs minimally.

All you have to do is select a single non-food item with a high markup and sell it at your cart. You know the things you see when you're in the supermarket checkout?

They cost a couple of dollars and you usually end up walking away with one or two of them? They usually cost around 1000 times their wholesale price (that is not a typo), and they're small ticket impulse items.

Some stores like convenience stores make most of their profits on these items. You can buy them wholesale online and 500 is usually a sufficient quantity to start with, so you can try an item out to see if there's any interest before you buy in bulk.

Stuff with high profit margins:

- Costume jewelry
- Key chains
- Cigarette lighters
- Maps

- Pens
- Seasonal items (for example, flags on the Fourth of July)
- Souvenirs

The profit margins on these items are much higher than on your food. In addition, they may attract some customers who weren't planning on buying food but get hungry when they smell your hot dogs. Similarly, people who are just there for lunch will get bored while they're waiting and will look at this stuff—many of them will end up buying some of it.

One of the best places to buy this stuff online is www.liquidation.com but you can even get it from your local dollar store, though not in huge quantities.

Now that you have a good idea on how to make your cart profitable, in the next step we'll talk about how to expand your business.

Step 14: How to Expand Your Business

When you follow all the steps above to set up your own successful hot dog cart, you'll realize what a great business it is and consider expanding. This can be a challenge because you can completely control your first cart, but to operate two or more you're going to need assistance.

The three ways of dealing with this are to take a partner, hire an employee to run a second cart, or lease out another cart.

Taking on a partner will mean revising your business structure and entering into a clear contract that specifies what each person will provide in terms of capital and sweat equity, and what they will get out of the business as well. This is the best way to expand if you have someone you really trust who is interested in your business, but even still the partnership needs to be formalized to avoid problems down the road.

Hiring someone to run the second cart preserves most of the profits for you. However, it comes with additional legal responsibilities such as unemployment insurance and withholding of income tax. You'll also have to have a backup plan for days when the employee fails to show up.

When you incorporated you should have gotten an employer identification number. You'll use this to file a federal payroll tax return, as well as W2s, W3s, and

W4s. You'll also need to fill out I-9s certifying that you are not employing illegal immigrants.

Having an employee also means that you'll need to inspect the cart from time to time to make sure he or she is running things properly. All of the details like collecting sales tax, performing accurate inventory checks and following food safety procedures will be left in this person's hands, but if they screw up, you're the one who pays the price. For this reason, you may prefer to lease your second cart.

When you lease a cart, you do everything in the above steps up until the business actually opens. It's your cart, but someone pays you to operate it. This can be either monthly rent or some percentage of their profits. The monthly rent is the better way to go if you're leasing your cart because you're guaranteed income no matter how your tenant runs their business.

Congratulations! If you've read this far you now know exactly how to operate a hot dog business. Step Fifteen is merely a summary of the previous steps in easy-to-read checklist format.

Step 15: Your Startup Checklist

We recommend that you read the whole guide through a few times before actually undergoing the steps, but this step presents a summary of everything that you can take with you while you're actually doing everything.

- Incorporate your business and apply for all other necessary permits, registrations and certifications.
- Find a commissary and get it approved by the health department.
- Get the regulations for a hot dog cart from your local health department.
- Pick out a cart that meets these regulations and bring them back to the health department for approval.
- Purchase your cart.
- Pick a location based on the criteria that has a lot of foot traffic and that you're easily visible and there's not too much competition.
- If your location is private property, negotiate permission and lease terms, if required.
- Buy food, packaging and other necessary supplies as well as the additional items you'll

need for your cart like a folding table, condiment holders and water tanks.

- Figure out your pricing.
- Do a dry run or two with friends and family to work out the kinks in serving and give yourself confidence.
- Follow proper food safety procedures.
- Find a small low-cost non-food item to sell at the hot dog stand to boost your profits.
- If you intend to expand, find a partner, an employee or a tenant for your second cart.

Congratulations! You are now ready to start your own hot dog business.

Recommended Resources

- HowExpert.com – Quick 'How To' Guides on All Topics from A to Z by Everyday Experts.
- HowExpert.com/free – Free HowExpert Email Newsletter.
- HowExpert.com/books – HowExpert Books
- HowExpert.com/courses – HowExpert Courses
- HowExpert.com/clothing – HowExpert Clothing
- HowExpert.com/membership – HowExpert Membership Site
- HowExpert.com/affiliates – HowExpert Affiliate Program
- HowExpert.com/writers – Write About Your #1 Passion/Knowledge/Expertise & Become a HowExpert Author.
- HowExpert.com/resources – Additional HowExpert Recommended Resources
- YouTube.com/HowExpert – Subscribe to HowExpert YouTube.
- Instagram.com/HowExpert – Follow HowExpert on Instagram.
- Facebook.com/HowExpert – Follow HowExpert on Facebook.

Made in United States
Orlando, FL
12 January 2022

13353267R00026